PIANO · VOCAL · GUITAR

Exalt His Name!

W9-CTG-651

ISBN 0-7935-5772-0

HAL•LEONARD
CORPORATION
7777 W. BLUEMOUND RD. P.O. BOX 13819 MILWAUKEE, WI 53213

Exalt His Name!

EASTER SONG

Words and Music by
ANNE HERRING

Brightly, in one

Hear the bells ring - ing, they're sing - ing, that
Hear the bells bells ring - ing, they're sing - ing, "Christ

we can be born a - gain! _____
is ris - en born from the dead!" _____

1

2

The _____

EXALT THE NAME

Words and Music by MARGARET BECKER
and MARK HAUTH

Moderately, with energy

walks up - on ___ the wind. ___ He rides a - bove ___ the storm. ___
rules the u - ni - verse, ___ yet hears the hum - ble cry, ___

Light - ning ___ flash - es from His
bring - ing com - fort ___ to the bro - ken

GETTING STRONGER

Words and Music by BOB CARLISLE
and CHARLIE PEACOCK

A FEW GOOD MEN

Words by SUSAN GAITHER JENNINGS
Music by BARRY JENNINGS

What this dy-ing world could use is a will-ing man of God who dares to go a-gainst the grain, and work with-out ap-plause, A man who'll raise the shield of faith pro-

FOR THE SAKE OF THE CALL

Words and Music by
STEVEN CURTIS CHAPMAN

Moderately Fast

We will a-ban-don it all For the sake of the call.

No oth-er rea-son at all, But the sake of the call.

Whol-ly de-vot-ed to live and to

THE GREAT ADVENTURE

Words and Music by STEVEN CURTIS CHAPMAN
and GEOFF MOORE

Sad-dle up your hors-es.

Start-ed out this morn...

THE GREAT DIVIDE

Words and Music by MATT HUESMANN
and GRANT CUNNINGHAM

Si - lence, trying to fath - om the dis - tance,

faith - ful. On my own I'm un - a - ble.

look - ing out 'cross the can - yon carved by

He found me hope - less, a - lone and sent a

HE COVERS ME

Moderately (with a half-time feel)

Words and Music by STEVE CAMP,
ROB FRAZIER and JOHN ROSASCO

Oh

Lord, I feel so bar - ren____ and a - shamed of who I am;
pres - sure builds a - round____ me____ and I feel a - bout to break,____

how I of - ten fell,____ I hid it well,____ it is a
I suf - fer pain - ful - ly____ from wrongs done to me but

HEAVEN IN THE REAL WORLD

Words and Music by
STEVEN CURTIS CHAPMAN

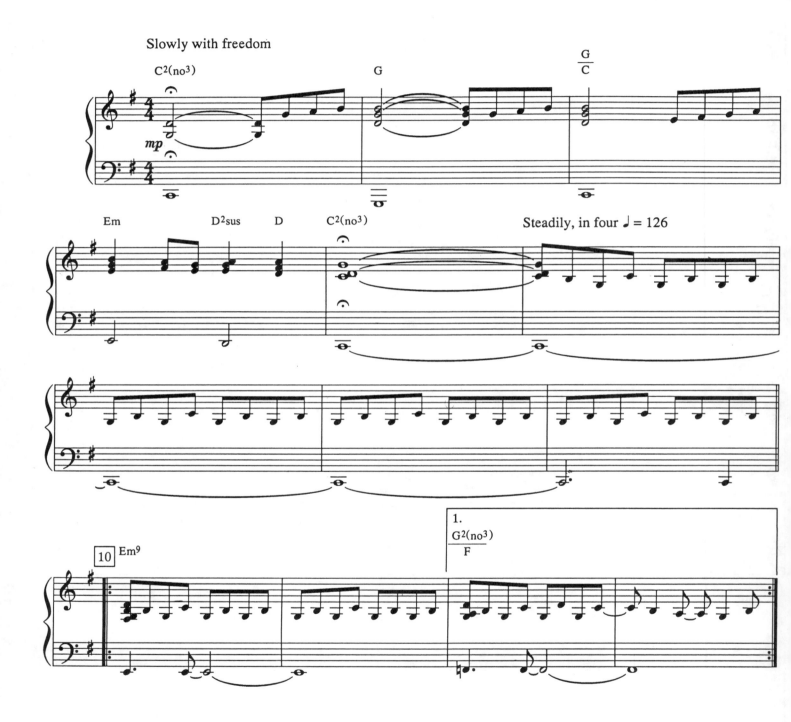

HERE IN MY HEART

Words and Music by SUSAN ASHTON
and GAYLA BORDERS

Moderately ♩ = 108

1. Won - d'ring, ___ Wait - ing, ___ — Rest - less ___ for a sign
2. Mean - ing, ___ Pur - pose, ___ Got lost in pur - suit ___ of my dreams.

Stronger feel: 2nd time

— I thought You walked ___ So slow. ___ In my haste,
— I've been long - ing, ___ Ach - ing, ___ In

IN A LITTLE WHILE

Words and Music by GARY CHAPMAN, BROWN BANNISTER,
AMY GRANT and SHANE KEISTER

1. Got a tick-et com-ing home, wish the of - fi - cer ___ had
2. Boy, that let-ter hit ___ the spot, made me think of all ___ I've

known ___ what a day to - day ___ has ___ been. ___
got, ___ and all that waits ___ for ___ me. ___

JESUS IS THE ANSWER

Words and Music by ANDRAÉ CROUCH
and SANDRA CROUCH

Je - sus is ___ the an - swer for the world ___ to - day. ___ A - bove Him there's ___ no oth - er, Je - sus is ___ the way. ___

JUBILEE

Words and Music by
MICHAEL CARD

KEEP MY MIND

Words and Music by
MARGARET BECKER

1. If wish - es did__
2. Some steps__ my feet__

I must live and breathe.
If it were up to me,
I'll nev - er cap -
I'd chain__ my - self

2nd time to CODA

- ture You,__ but a - You could cap - ture me.
__ to You__ and

Keep my mind__ on high - er things,____
Keep my mind__ on truth.__

Keep my mind__ on the an - chor of love____ that

MORE TO THIS LIFE

Words and Music by STEVEN CURTIS CHAPMAN
and PHIL NAIS

than this life—— a - lone—— can be.——

More to—— this life,—

—— more to this

life. More to—this life.——

(optional "live" ending)

Repeat ad lib. and fade slowly

PEOPLE KEEP WRITING HIM SONGS

Words and Music
PHILL McHUG

THE ONE I'VE BEEN WAITING FOR

Words and Music by CHRISTINE DENTÉ
and CHARLIE PEACOCK

breath - ing_ new_ life_ in - to me! ___

Ha _____ Ha_

Dreams do_ come _true. I've been wait - ing, wait - ing for ___

SO MANY BOOKS

This song was written in Beijing during a Bible smuggling trip with members of the Bible League.
It is dedicated to all the courageous men and women, the teachers and pastors, who labor for the kingdom in China.

Words and Music by
MICHAEL CARD

Energetic feel in four ♩ = 126

1. There
(2. There'll)

____ is a hun - ger, a long - ing for bread,___ And so___ comes the call___ for the poor___ to be fed.___ More hun -
____ come a time,___ the pro - phets would say,___ When the joy of man - kind___ will be with - ered a - way.___ A want,

towards the Light.

2. There'll __ -pen a Bi - ble and move __ towards the Light, __ O -

- pen a Bi - ble and move __ towards the Light. __ The Word __ won't go out __ ex - cept __

__ it re - turn __ Full, __ o - ver - flow - ing. And so __ we must learn. _____

SAY THE NAME

Words and Music by MARGARET BECK
and CHARLIE PEACO

SERVE THE LORD

By CARMAN

THIS TOWN

Words and Music by STEVE CAM...
CAROL FRAZIER and ROB FRAZI...

This old **town** __
Look out - **side** your

may not **mean** __ that **much** __ to **you,** __
back door, **tell** __ me **what** __ you **see.** __

you?

He will lead us ___ to ho - li - er ways, ___ to a foun -

WAITING FOR YOUR LOVE TO COME DOWN

Words and Music by JEFF BORDERS
and GAYLA BORDERS

WISE UP

Words and Music by BILLY SIMON
and WAYNE KIRKPATRICK

Laid back double time rock ♩ = 102

1. Got my-self __ in this sit-u-a-tion I'm not sure __ a-bout, __ climb-in' in __ where there's temp-ta-tion.

2. Take a look _ at your in-ten-tions,

when you have _ to choose, _ could it be _ that ap-pre-hen-sion

might be tell-in' you _ to You've got to wise up,

D.S. al Coda 𝄋

you've got to think twice, you've got to wise up, you've got to, you've got to

The Finest In Inspirational Music

America's Gospel Top Forty
40 of the most popular gospel songs ever to hit the Gospel Top Forty, including: God Bless The U.S.A. • I Bowed On My Knees And Cried Holy • More Than Wonderful • Somebody Touched Me • many more. Arranged for piano/guitar/4-part vocal.
00359061 ....$8.95

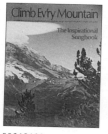

Climb Ev'ry Mountain
Over 130 songs: Day By Day • One Day At A Time • Bridge Over Troubled Water • Let There Be Peace On Earth • Gonna Build A Mountain • The Old Rugged Cross • Rock Of Ages • Abide With Me • Nearer, My God, To Thee • What A Friend We Have In Jesus.
00312100 ....$16.95

Country Gospel U.S.A.
50 songs written for piano/ guitar/four-part vocal. Highlights: Daddy Sang Bass • He Set Me Free • I Saw The Light • Kum Ba Yah • Mansion Over The Hilltop • Love Lifted Me • Turn Your Radio On • When The Saints Go Marching In • many others.
00240139 ....$9.95

Favorite Hymns
71 all-time favorites, including: Abide With Me • Amazing Grace • Ave Maria • Christ The Lord Is Risen Today • Faith Of Our Fathers • In The Sweet By And By • Jesus Loves Me! • Just A Closer Walk With Thee • A Mighty Fortress Is Our God • Onward Christian Soldiers • Rock Of Ages • Swing Low, Sweet Chariot • Were You There? • and many more!
00490436 ....$12.95

Glorious Praise
Great Songwriters & Songs
24 songs, including: Find A Way • Friends • How Majestic Is Your Name • O Magnify The Lord • Via Dolorosa • The Warrior Is A Child.
00359895 ....$10.95

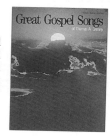

Great Gospel Songs Of Thomas A. Dorsey
37 of his greatest songs, including: There'll Be Peace In The Valley (For Me) • Take My Hand Precious Lord • Say A Little Prayer For Me • Someway, Somehow, Sometime, Somewhere • There Is No Friend Like Jesus.
00359946 ....$7.95

Gregorian Chant
This centuries-old art form is regaining popularity as people discover its free-flowing rhythms and haunting melodies. This one-of-a-kind collection includes 23 beautiful and celestial plainchants for a capella voice.
00310003 ....$8.95

The New Illustrated Family Hymn Book
Featuring designs from the Hallmark Collection
A collector's edition for everyone who loves hymns. This deluxe album features a history of the hymn from its Old Testament origins and 50 of the world's most popular hymns for piano, organ or electronic keyboard. Each hymn is presented with an account of its history and a magnificent four-color design selected from the archives of Hallmark Cards. The greatest Christian hymns are included, such as: Abide With Me • Amazing Grace • How Great Thou Art • In The Garden • The Old Rugged Cross • What A Friend We Have In Jesus. Includes 50 full-color photos!
00183297 ....$19.95

Favorites Of Mahalia Jackson
15 favorites of the world's greatest gospel singer: Amazing Grace • God Spoke To Me One Day • I Can Put My Trust In Jesus • Move On Up A Little Higher • What Could I Do If It Wasn't For The Lord? • more. Includes biography.
00307150 ....$5.95

The New Young Messiah
Matching folio to the album featuring top Contemporary Christian artists performing a modern rendition of Handel's *Messiah*. Features Sandy Patty, Steven Curtis Chapman, Larnelle Harris, and others.
00310006 ....$16.95

Our God Reigns
50 classics, including: Awesome God • El Shaddai • He Will Carry You • How Majestic Is Your Name • Jesus Is The Answer • O Magnify The Lord • Say The Name • Thank You • Via Dolorosa • and more.
00311695 ....$17.95

Praise
25 selections: Behold The Lamb • El Shaddai • How Majestic Is Your Name • Praise The Lord • Sweet, Sweet Spirit • Through His Eyes • Worthy The Lamb • many more.
00240775 ....$8.95

Songs Of Worship And Praise
18 songs, including: El Shaddai • How Majestic Is Your Name • The King Of Who I Am • There's Something About That Name • Worthy The Lamb.
00361131 ....$7.95

Gospel
The Ultimate Series
A collection of 100 of the most inspirational gospel songs ever, featuring: Because He Lives • Climb Ev'ry Mountain • Daddy Sang Bass • Everything Is Beautiful • For Loving Me • He • He Touched Me • He's Got The Whole World In His Hands • His Eye Is On The Sparrow • Home Where I Belong • How Great Thou Art • I Saw The Light • Just A Closer Walk With Thee • Just Any Day Now • Kum Ba Yah • Mansion Over The Hilltop • Old Rugged Cross • Peace In The Valley • Put Something Back • Rock Of Ages • Sincerely Yours • The Singer • The Sun's Coming Up • Take My Hand, Precious Lord • Without Him • more.
00241009 ....$17.95

FOR MORE INFORMATION, SEE YOUR LOCAL MUSIC DEALER, OR WRITE TO:

HAL•LEONARD™ CORPORATION
7777 W. BLUEMOUND RD. P.O. BOX 13819 MILWAUKEE, WI 53213

Prices, contents, and availability subject to change without notice.
Some products may not be available outside the U.S.A.